THE YEAR
PORTF∞LIO
IN CANADIAN CARICATURE

ALLOW ME

CONS♛TITUTION

Edited by Guy Badeaux

CROC
PUBLISHING

THE AUTHOR

GUY BADEAUX is the editorial page cartoonist for *Le Droit* in Ottawa.

THE PUBLISHER

CROC is a humor magazine very famous in Québec that deals irreverently in all matters, delves in parody and is written in a funny language. This book is the third in a collection that we hope to publish long enough to start worrying about how to incorporate the number 9 in **PORTFOOLIO** when we reach the 90's.

PORTFOOLIO 87, THE YEAR IN CANADIAN CARICATURE

ISBN: 2-920341-19-7

© 1987 Ludcom Inc. First edition
No part of this book may be reproduced or distributed in any form or by any means without prior written permission of the publisher.

Ludcom Inc., 5800 Monkland, Montréal, H4A 1G1

Cover by Duncan MacPherson
Colour by Cam Cardow
Back-cover by Andy Donato
Design by Michel Durand

Dépôt légal: troisième trimestre 1987;
Bibliothèque Nationale du Québec.

ACKNOWLEDGEMENTS

I would like to thank all the cartoonists involved for making this book possible. I am especially indebted to all those who showed up in Ottawa this summer for helping in the selection of the drawings. I am especially indebted to Janet Desbarats and Charles Gordon, without whose assistance I probably wouldn't have met my deadline.

G.B.

PLUGS

Since you will enjoy this book, here is a list of some of our contributors' latest publications:

AISLIN: *Old Whores* / McClelland and Stewart. $14.95

Stanley BURKE and Roy PETERSON: *Swamped* / Douglas & McIntyre. $10.95

DONATO: *The Strife of Brian* / Key Porter Books: $9.95

GABLE: *The Editorial Cartoons of Brian Gable* / Western Producer Prairie Books: $9.95

GIRERD: *Le meilleur de Girerd '86* / Éditions La Presse: $14.95

KRIEGER and Marjorie NICHOLS: *Bill Bennett: The End* / Douglas & McIntyre. $8.95

WICKS: *The Second Ben Wicks Treasury* / Methuen: $14.95

National Newspaper Award 1986

Brian Gable, *Regina Leader Post,* January 31, 1986

National Business Writing Award 1986

Today's Youth

Guy Badeaux, *Le Droit,* January 7, 1986

THE CREATURE FROM MEECH LAKE

Just when the First Ministers thought the coast was clear, and that Quebec was finally happy, and that the whole constitutional debate was put to bed – a creature from the past came back to haunt them...

PICTURE THEM ALL IN A BOAT ON A RIVER,
WITH TANGERINE TREES AND MARMALADE SKIES...

Jenkins, *The Globe and Mail*

OKAY,
WE'RE **IN**....

WHEN CAN WE
START
OPTING **OUT** ?

Re-inventing Federalism

Rodewalt, *Calgary Herald*

Franklin, *The Globe and Mail*

Cummings, *The Winnipeg Free Press*

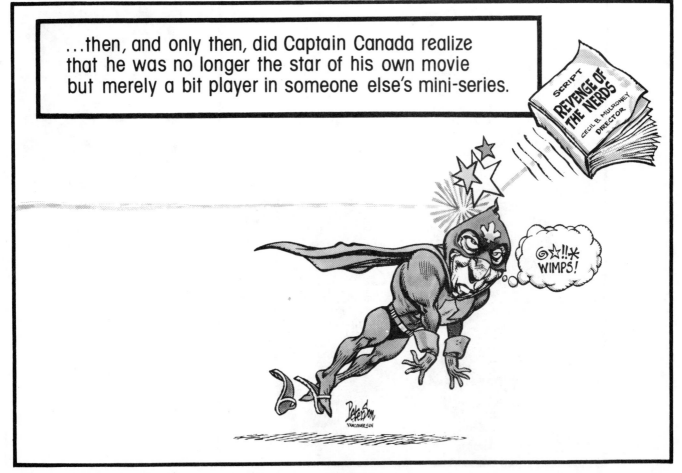

...then, and only then, did Captain Canada realize that he was no longer the star of his own movie but merely a bit player in someone else's mini-series.

WELCOME TO CANADA!

While the welcome mat was put out for Quebec, the rug was pulled out from under refugees. One year after Tamils landed in Newfoundland, Parliament was summoned for an emergency debate on immigration policy...

"...SORRY... BUT FORM 1146-B SPECIFICALLY REQUESTS AT LEAST **TWO** CERTIFIABLE
INCIDENTS OF POLITICAL OPPRESSION..."

Cummings, *The Winnipeg Free Press*

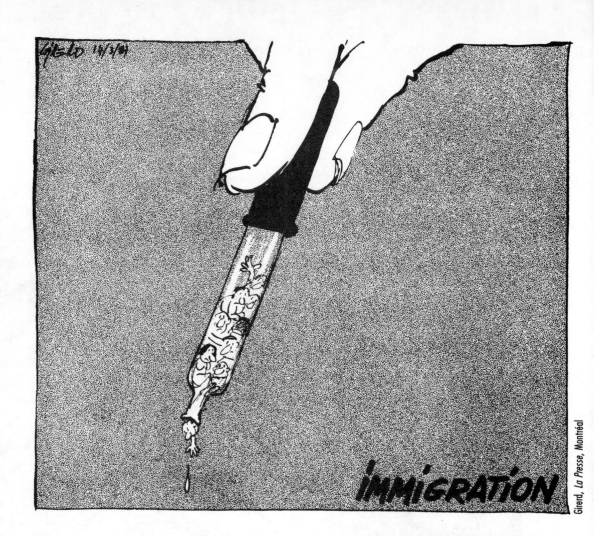

IMMIGRATION

Girerd, *La Presse, Montréal*

Elston, *Calgary Sun*

Roschkov, *The Edmonton Sun*

Jenkins, *The Globe and Mail*

From here on we have two choices: the Tamils' route, via Newfoundland, or the Sikhs' route, via Nova Scotia.

"Taxi!"

Gaboury, Le Soleil, Québec

Jenkins, *The Globe and Mail*

DOWN IN SALVADOR

Roschkov, *The Edmonton Sun*

Mackinnon, *The Halifax Herald*

DEATH PENALTY

While we were trying to slam the door shut on refugees and immigrants, our politicians were opening, yet again, the Pandora's Box of debate on capital punishment.

At the instigation of the "hang 'em high, and hang 'em often" section of the Tory bleachers, MPs agonized (at great length, if not with great eloquence) philosophically over the death penalty.

Our abolitionists managed to keep the vigilantes at bay – at least until the next redneck uprising.

Cummings, *The Winnipeg Free Press*

Mackinnon, *The Halifax Herald*

CAPITAL PUNISHMENT QUIZ...

CAN YOU SPOT THE TORY BACK-BENCHER?

Constable, *Union Art Services*

Are you for or against the death penalty?

Bado, Erratum

I am for the death penalty.

Girerd, La Presse, Montréal   February 11, 1975, rerun.

"The Mood of the Public Swings from decade to decade".

Bierman, *Monday, Victoria*

MULRONEY

Dalton Camp was hired to improve the PM's image. The Emperor had no clothes, was slipping drastically in the polls, but, on the other hand, was wearing beautiful shoes. Gucci loafers, in fact. A closet full.

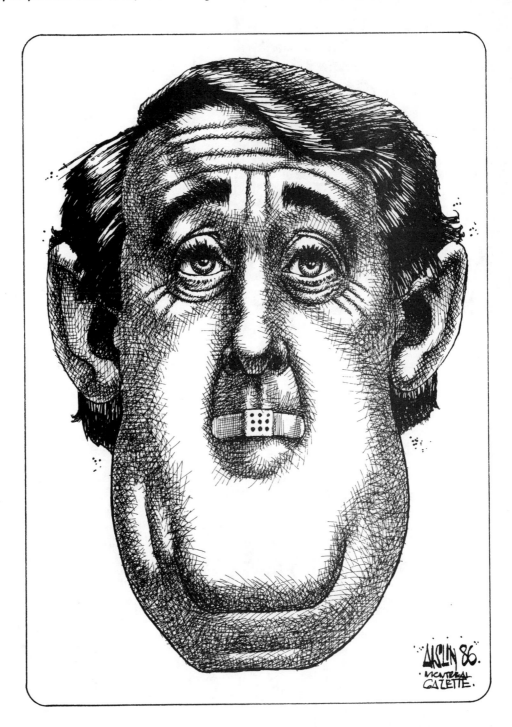

PROFILES IN POWER ——

Cummings, *The Winnipeg Free Press*

I LOVE IT, MAVIS — BRIAN IS FINALLY FIGHTING BACK —

—NO MORE REPEATING ERRORS—NO MORE CONTRADICTORY STATEMENTS

WHAT'S HE DONE NOW?

MAZANKOWSKI WILL SPEAK FOR HIM

THAT SHOULD STOP THE NAME CALLING

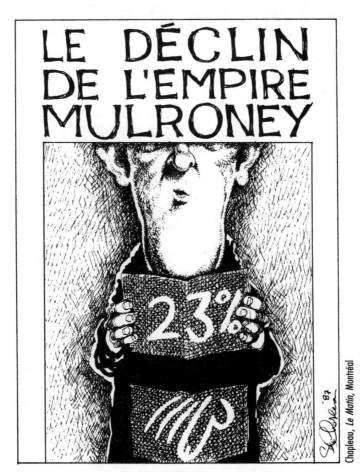

The Blues Brothers

"THANKS, MOM."

LOOK —
I THINK THINGS
ARE ABOUT TO
TURN AROUND —

— SURE WE'VE BEEN
UNDER THE GUN —
SURE WE'VE HAD
SOME TOUGH
MOMENTS —

— AT TIMES THINGS
HAVE GOTTEN A
LITTLE OUT OF
HAND —
I'D BE THE...

BRIAN —
STOP TALKING
HIS EAR OFF
AND LET THE
BABY GO TO
SLEEP

Brian's dilemma...

POLLS

...eighty-four pairs, and no climbing boots!

100 PAIRS OF SHOES?!!

BOY...MILA MUST BE HUNGRY!

...I SHALL GO TO THE WEST AND LIFT THEIR SPIRITS BY CLARIFYING OUR PLANS AND PROPOSALS HERE IN OTTAWA!

...NOW, JUST OFF OUR MASTER BEDROOM WE'RE PROPOSING A MAUVE SILK BROCADE...

TORIES

During the last election campaign, Mulroney promised Canadians the moon, but he could only come up with a jail for his riding.

Port Cartier was supposed to bring prosperity to Manicouagan, but otherwise the Tories weren't as fortunate. One has to think of: Sinclair Stevens, Roch LaSalle, André Bissonette, Erik Nielsen, Michel Gravel...

"LET'S FACE IT, THERE'S NO WHORE LIKE AN OLD WHORE". BRIAN MULRONEY-JULY 14, 1984.

MS. FEBRUARY.

TORY OF THE MONTH.

AISLIN 87.
MONTREAL GAZETTE

OFFICIAL SALUTES

VULCAN   BOY SCOUT   CABINET MINISTER

Constable, *Union Art Services*

THE TORY HANDSHAKE —

Cummings, *The Winnipeg Free Press*

"YA DANCE
WITH THE LADY
WHAT BRUNG YA"...

THE ROAD TO PROSPERITY.

MANICOUAGAN
10 KM

Nave
edmonton
journal

"This time, to keep it all fair, we're going to be Tories . . ."

...AND NOW A FEW PARTING WORDS FROM ERIK NIELSEN...

ERIK NIELSEN'S MEMOIRS...

I was born in

After leaving the Air Force I

My years in Parliament were marked by

Anything left to hide, Mr. Stevens?   Oh! So little.

According to the Conservative MP from Kitchener, Quebecers have corrupt political practices.

How are we so different from other Canadians?

JOHN & ED

Canadians witnessed two "firsts" this year: Liberals stabbing themselves in the back and the NDP leading in the polls.

What's going on here? The Liberals seem to be behaving like Tories, and the NDP like Liberals...

OFFICE FURNITURE...

`the MULRONEY´
(PRESIDENTIAL STYLE)

`the BROADBENT´
(Suitable for waiting rooms)

`the TURNER´
(98 positions)

UNION MADE IN CANADA

Pritchard/87 STAR PHOENIX-SASKATOON-

MA POSITION EST CLAIRE!

My position is clear!

BADO, Le Droit, Ottawa

EUGENE "WAILING"

Mackinnon, *The Halifax Herald*

A *RELIEVED* JOHN TURNER

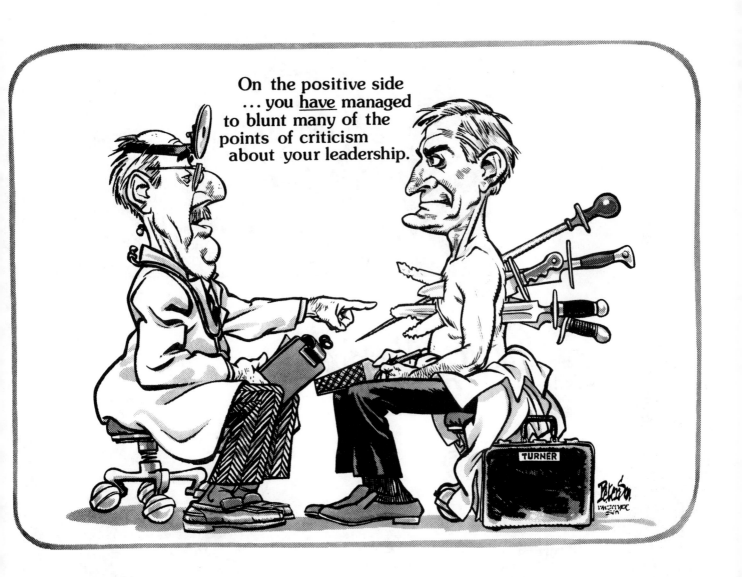

The
Iacocca ~ Broadbent
Summit:

IF POLLS RULED...

The NDP according to the Tories...

THE PROVINCES

Western Canada suffered a series of blows. Trade wars hurt Western farmers. Governments were re-elected in B.C. and Saskatchewan. Manitoba lost the F-18 maintenance contract to Montreal, and the Winnipeg Blue Bombers to the Eastern Conference of the CFL. Not that the East liked having the Blue Bombers all that much. The Bombers were the only Blue Machine to win anything in the East.

CAM, *The Ottawa Citizen*

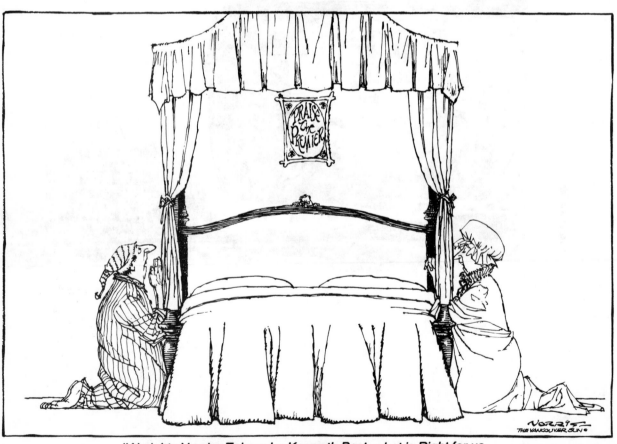

"Almighty Vander Zalm, who Knoweth Best what is Right for us,
Govern and Direct us in Thy Path of Righteousness . . ."

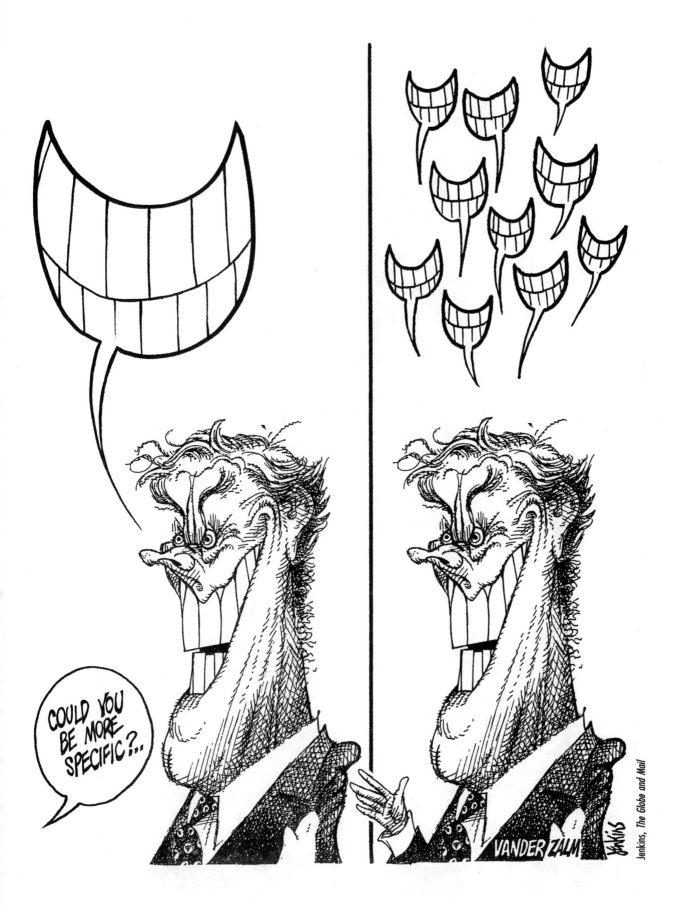

Roschkov, *The Edmonton Sun*

YOHO NATIONAL PARK

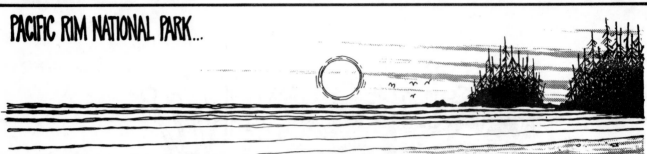

PACIFIC RIM NATIONAL PARK...

SOUTH MORESBY PROVINCIAL PARK

Victoria Times-Colonist RAESIDE

OK, FEDS, MORE DOUGH OR DA TREE GETS IT!

B.C.

SOUTH MORESBY HELD TO RANSOM.

TIMBER!

B.C. SPEECH FROM THE THRONE

Jenkins, *The Globe and Mail*

THEIR NUMBERS ONCE COVERED THE PRAIRIES....

DITTO.

1936

...HOPE IT RAINS, MARTHA.

1986

...HOPE THE EUROPEAN AGRICULTURAL ECONOMISTS CAN INFLUENCE A REDUCTION IN PRIME SECTOR SUBSIDIES ALLOWING IN TURN THE U.S. SENATE SUB-COMMITTE TO RECOMMEND A CONTINGENT REDUCTION IN RURAL EQUITY ENHANCEMENT PROGRAMS, EASING DOMESTIC PRICING TRENDS, MARTHA.

Chapleau, *Le Devoir*, Montréal

QUESTION DE LANGUE

Chapleau, *Le Devoir*, Montréal

BADO, *Le Droit*, Ottawa

We want a revolution inside the system!
Now that we control the government, we will politicize the status quo and bring up our children as true patriots...

I want a revolutionary system!
A Bang & Olufsen sound system with compact disk and remote control; a stereo tv and digital recorder for my BMW...

Pier, *Le Journal de Montréal*

Gaboury, *Le Soleil, Québec*

After all, Christianity had its martyrs,
why not the CNTU?

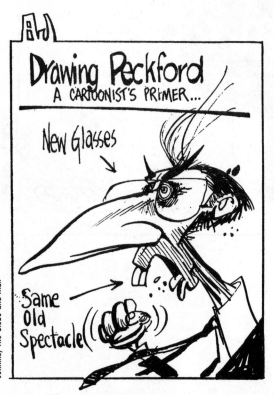

Jenkins, *The Globe and Mail*

FREE TRADE

The U.S. slapped a 15% duty on softwood lumber. We retaliated by slapping it on ourselves instead. It made as much sense as anything else in a free trade debate.

Despite striking a quick deal with Mexico on acid rain, the U.S. government felt that still more research was needed in our case.

Speaking of unfinished business: the Dome sale was still up in the air; tax reform was half-finished; and the submarines were still on the drawing-board.

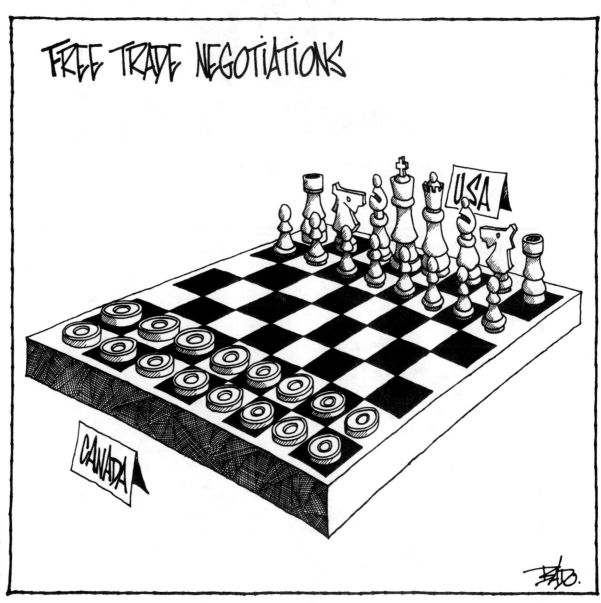

SURROGATE
MOTHER of
THE YEAR

SOFT WOOD...

FREE TIRADE DIALOGUE

'Hear somethin'? . . . No, I didn't hear somethin' . . . Why, did YOU hear somethin', Simon?'

" I'm prepared to have American culture on the table and have it damaged by Canadian influence..."
CLAYTON YEUTTER

RAMBO

ANNE OF GREEN GABLES

Acid rain

PLUIES ACIDES...

CANADA

Delatti, *Le Nouvelliste*, Trois-Rivières

NEWS ITEM: MEXICO REACHES AGREEMENT WITH U.S. ON ACID RAIN...

NOW WE KNOW HOW TO DEAL WITH THE AMERICANS!

BADO, *Le Droit*, Ottawa

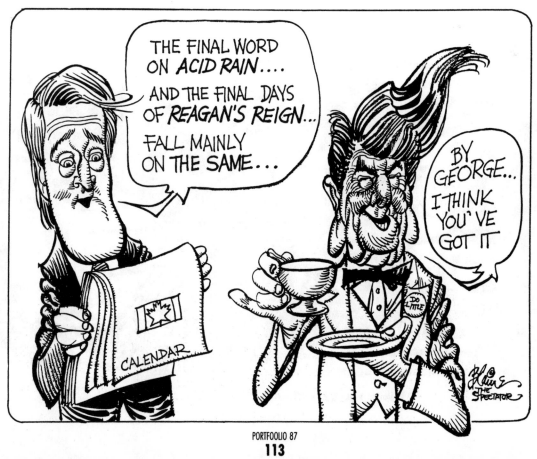

"WHEN YOU'RE BOUGHT, YOU'RE HOT..."

"... We've got to reduce our liquid equity earning ratio... by splitting our mid term spousal transfer withdrawal RRIFs and bypassing short term mutual GDRS warrants accrual, we simply arrive in a safe, highly liquid, lock up earnings reimbursement stance... thus reducing our GIC maturity futures tax... okay...?"

Jenkins, *The Globe and Mail*

"... I left my brief case on the bus and I'm lost without my notes... I can't remember, is Canprov taking over Transcam and Nordev or is it Nordev taking over Silcan and Candome... and who is Tormont taking over...?"

Franklin, *The Globe and Mail*

Gaboury, *Le Soleil*, Québec

GENUINE ESKIMO CARVING

EDWARDS
The Whig-Standard

'You can't imagine how relieved we were to hear that the government might be spending billions of dollars to build submarines that will protect us from the Americans.'

BEDTIME FOR BONZO

Was Nancy running the Contras? Or Ollie North? Was **anybody** running Ollie North? Was Reagan a Teflon man or a lame duck? How lame were the Contras? How many guns would you have to sell to Iran to make Teflon Contras? And what did Fawn Hall have to do with any of this? Tune in and find out...

Franklin, *The Globe and Mail*

Chapleau, *Le Matin*, Montréal

"THAT'S WHAT I'VE BEEN SAYING ALL ALONG."

Kamienski, *The Winnipeg Sun*

AMERICAN HERO —

LT. COL. O. NORTH

Cummings, *The Winnipeg Free Press*

Cummings, The Winnipeg Free Press

...so Nancy suggested we get someone new and credible in the cabinet... someone who really knows how to handle U.S. foreign affairs policy. Interested?

"GRANTED, SOME CONCESSIONS WERE MADE TO IRAN."

ALL THE PRESIDENT'S MEN....

Richards '86
STAR-PHOENIX-SASKATOON-

"Dear Ron, we need 100 million
bucks to overthrow our leader...
no... make that 'commie' leader."

TEFLON
WARRANTY

Jenkins, *The Globe and Mail*

VIOLENCE

Next to the violence inflicted by the real experts of the world, Canadian violence was kid stuff. Still, the Canadian version was interesting in its own way. Some of it you could even follow in the sports pages. Some of it went to the dogs.

HOW TO RECOGNIZE SOME OF THE DIFFERENT FACTIONS IN BEIRUT....

ISLAMIC JIHAD

SHIITE AMAL MOVEMENT

HIZBALLAH (PARTY OF GOD)

PALESTINIAN LIBERATION ORGANIZATION

PALESTINIAN REVENGE ORGANIZATION

JUSTICE AND REVENGE FRONT

ISLAMIC RESISTANCE FRONT

SYRIA

...THE POPULAR FRONT TO FREE UPPER VOLTA...

"There's no answer...I think we've taken everyone hostage."

"Oh, Ahmad, isn't it exciting? Our first visit to Paris."

It's only because France protected me against the
Shah that I took so few hostages!

... And look how France repays us.

"Couldn't we get rid of apartheid and call it something else?"

"Have you any idea how miserable your life will be if they bring in sanctions against South Africa?"

And the winner is...

Franklin, *The Globe and Mail*

The white man's shadow.

L'OMBRE DU BLANC

Girerd, *La Presse, Montréal*

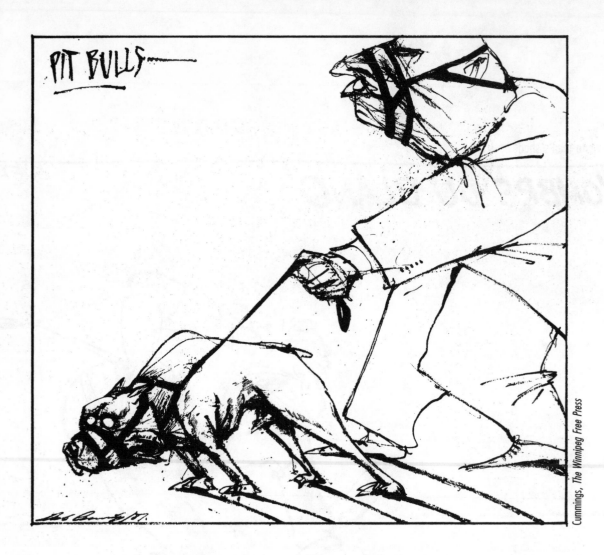

PIT BULLS —

WALDHEIM

" I'VE HAD IT UP TO HERE WITH THESE FALSE ACCUSATIONS."

Pinochet takes Communion.

Girard, *La Presse*, Montréal

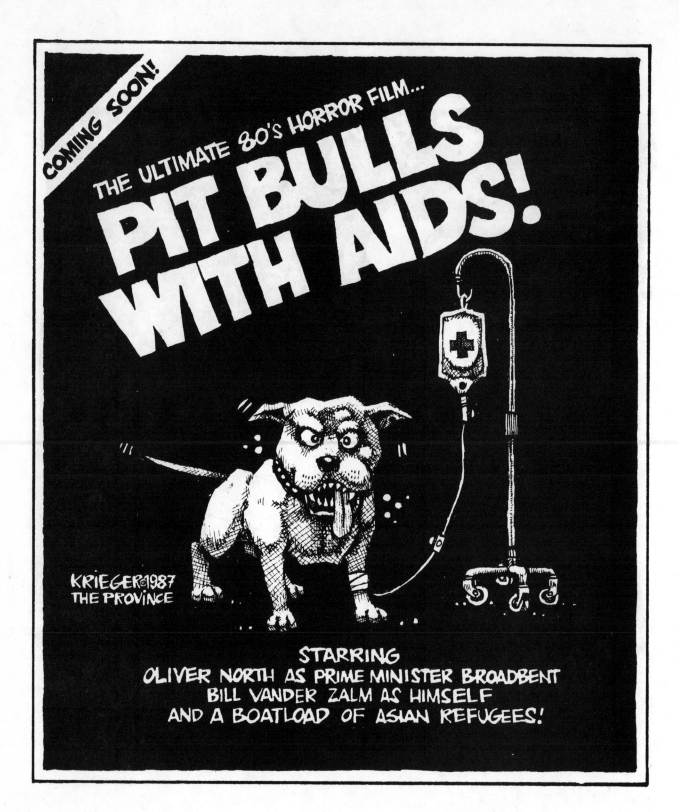

HOCKEY NIGHT IN CANADA

JTTODD'87©

U.S.A

Canada

SATURDAY NIGHT SPECIALS

A MODEST PROPOSAL FOR THE RESTORATION OF CAPITAL PUNISHMENT

SEX IN OUR TIMES

We had preachers in heat, secretaries in centerfolds, Marines and mascara, salvation and scandals, condoms and commandments, surrogates and censors.

Re-write the sex manuals; burn your old Playboys; marry a Catholic; don't run for the Presidency, and – above all – remember that laughter can be orgasmic.

Bierman, *Monday, Victoria*

"Is yours a boy or a girl?"

Cummings, *The Winnipeg Free Press*

MECHANICS OF BILL
C-54 EXPLAINED

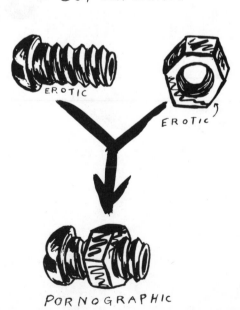

EROTIC

EROTIC

PORNOGRAPHIC

Constable, *Union Art Services*

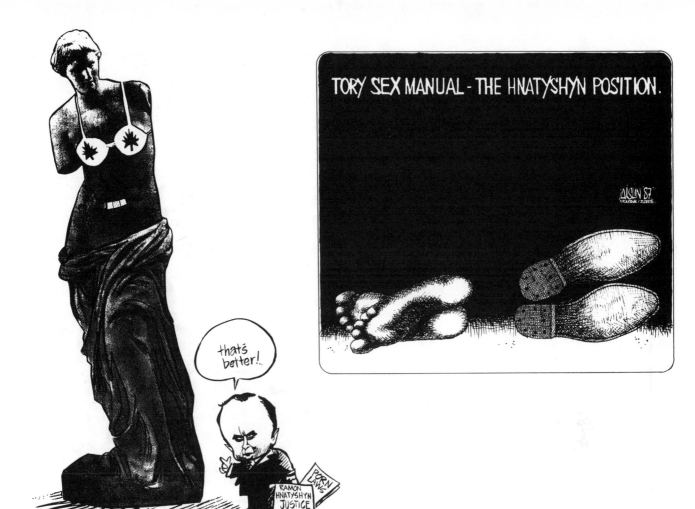

'So I've told Mary Lou she can go out with that young man just as long as he's not a preacher, a marine or a presidential candidate.'

Dumbo.

MISCELLANY

The Senate flexed its muscles, so did the postal workers, and of course, Rick Hansen.

Canada Post cut back services, as did the CBC, and smokers were urged to cut down.

And we can all go to bed secure in the knowledge that things can only be worse tomorrow...

Kamienski, *The Winnipeg Sun*

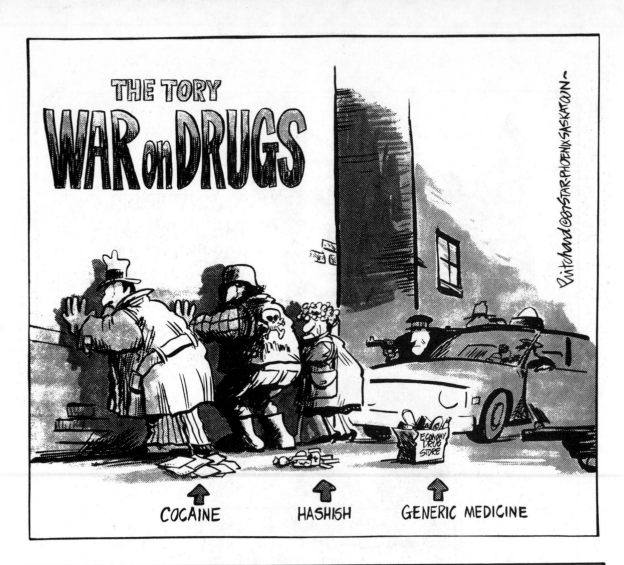

'On certain questions they should heed our expert advice.'

Birth of a Legend

...STREAMLINING THE OPERATION.

NEW GOVERNMENT PROPOSALS TO REGULATE MEDIA REPORTING OF OPINION POLLS WILL MAKE IT DIFFICULT FOR THE ELECTRONIC MEDIA TO REPORT THE RESULTS OF THE POLLS IN SHORT CLIPS.

HERE ARE THREE POSSIBLE WAYS THE MEDIA MAY SNEAK IN POLL RESULTS IF THE LEGISLATION IS PASSED...

IN TRAFFIC REPORTS...

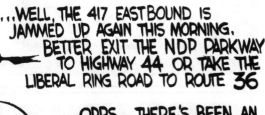

...WELL, THE 417 EASTBOUND IS JAMMED UP AGAIN THIS MORNING. BETTER EXIT THE NDP PARKWAY TO HIGHWAY 44 OR TAKE THE LIBERAL RING ROAD TO ROUTE 36

...OPPS...THERE'S BEEN AN ACCIDENT ON THE TORY EXPRESS... BETTER TAKE THE OFF-RAMP AT HIGHWAY 22

CAM

IN SPORTS...

THE BLUE JAYS HAMMERED THE YANKEES 7-3 ...THE NDP WALTZED PAST THE GRITS 44-36

...AND THE TORIES LOST BY 22 POINTS IN A GAME PLAYED AGAINST THEMSELVES

THE WEATHER... THE NDP...SUNNY WITH A HIGH OF 44 THE LIBERALS WILL SEE A HIGH OF 36 UNDER UNSETTLED SKIES ...AND THE CONSERVATIVES REACH 22 IN RAIN FOLLOWED BY PLAGUES AND EARTHQUAKES

CAM, The Ottawa Citizen

COMING UP AT ELEVEN, WE'LL HAVE A REPORT ON THE LATEST ROUND OF C.B.C. BUDGET CUTS...

...IF THE FILM IS BACK FROM THE DRUGSTORE BY THEN.

AND IF THE CAMERA IS OUT OF PAWN.

Victoria Times-Colonist.

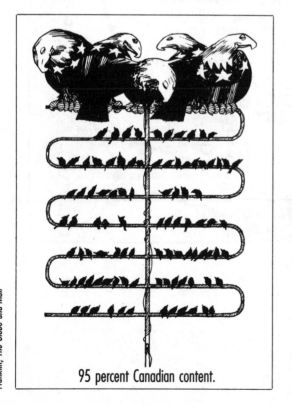

95 percent Canadian content.

IF MULRONEY HAD HANDLED THE RESEARCH GRANTS...

WATER?!! YOU WANT WATER, ARCHIMEDES?.. WHAT'S NEXT, FREE SOAP?!!

LISTEN, GALILEO..., I KNOW YOU CAN DO THIS WITH JUST ONE WEIGHT...

"Smoking, non-smoking or trying to quit?"

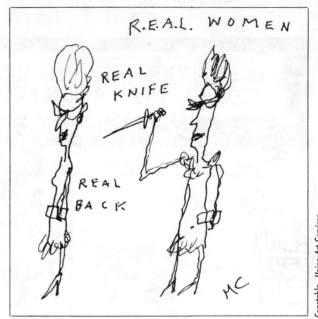

R.E.A.L. WOMEN

REAL KNIFE

REAL BACK

MC

Constable, Union Art Services

EQUAL PAY FOR WORK OF EQUAL VALUE...

CLERK TYPIST = WAREHOUSEMAN

WIDGIT MAKER = COMPUTER ASSEMBLER

BRITCHMAN @ '86 STAR PHOENIX · SASKATOON ·

POLITICIAN = MANURE SPREADER

... would you like to feel my biceps...?

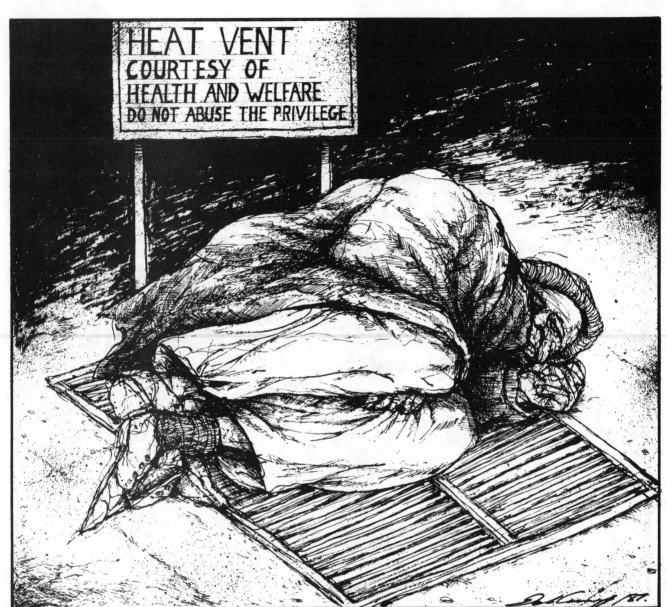

BIOGRAPHIES

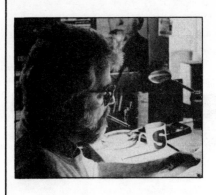

Aislin is the name of **Terry Mosher**'s eldest daughter and the *nom de plume* he uses as the editorial page cartoonist for *the Gazette* in Montréal. Syndicated by *The Toronto Star,* he has freelanced in the U.S. and abroad for such publications as *The New York Times, Time Magazine, The National Lampoon, Harper's, The Atlantic Monthly* and *Punch Magazine.* Born in Ottawa in 1941, he is a graduate of Quebec City's École des Beaux-Arts. Aislin has won a number of citations including two Canadian National Newspaper Awards (1977 and 1978), the prestigious Quill Award... "for outstanding contributions to the flow of public information on Canadian affairs," and five individual prizes from The International Salon of Caricature. In May of 1985, Aislin was the youngest person ever to be inducted into The Canadian News Hall of Fame.

Bado is **Guy Badeaux**'s last name pronounced phonetically. Born in Montréal in 1949, he worked there, left and right, for a wide spectrum of publications before moving to Ottawa in 1981 to become the editorial page cartoonist of *Le Droit.* President of the Association of Canadian Cartoonists, he won the 1986 National Business Writing Award for political cartooning.

Born in Toronto in 1917, **Sid Barron** moved to Victoria with his family as a very young child. In 1959 he took a crack at drawing editorial page cartoons for *The Victoria Times* and two years later joined *The Toronto Star* where he was hired by Pierre Berton. Barron has had an on-and-off working relationship with the paper ever since.

"... now this art I can understand... he's painting real people...!"

Josh Beutel was born and educated in Montréal, Québec. He majored in drawing and painting, graduating from Sir George Williams University (now Concordia U.) in 1966. He taught Art in high schools in Ontario and Labrador while freelancing political cartoons for various weekly and daily newspapers. Since the Autumn of 1978, Josh Beutel has been the cartoonist for the Saint John (New Brunswick) *Telegraph-Journal* and *Evening Times-Globe*. His work is syndicated in the U.S. and Europe by Rothco Cartoons Inc. Cartoons of his have been published in *Newsweek, The Financial Post, New York Times, Chicago Tribune, World Press Review, London Observer,* and other publications, as well as in a number of textbooks and collections of political cartooning. Josh Beutel has produced three books, *Cartoons by Beutel* (1981), *Best of Beutel* (1983), and *Say Goodnight, Dick,* A Collection of Hatfield Cartoons (1985).

Born in Amsterdam in 1921, **Bob Bierman** did some work for various Dutch publications after the war before emigrating to Canada in 1950. First working as a bar doorman in Toronto, he soon moved west to BC. In 1954, he published his first cartoon in *The Victoria Times*. In June of 1978 he drew a cartoon of then Human Resources Minister Bill Vander Zalm pulling wings off flies, which was printed by the *Times*. Vander Zalm successfully sued the *Times* and Bierman for libel but the decision was overturned by the Supreme Court. He has, since 1976, been working on a regular basis for *Monday* in Victoria and recently started his own syndication.

Blaine was born in Glace Bay, Nova Scotia. He has been the editorial page cartoonist of the Hamilton *Spectator* since 1961. Winner of the National Newspaper Award in 1974 and again in 1982, he is the only Canadian cartoonist to win the coveted Reuben Award in New York (1970). First winner of the Grand Prize at Montreal's International Salon of Cartoons in 1965, Blaine has also freelanced for *The New York Times, Time* and *Playboy*. A black-belt instructor in karate, he also writes music and sings.

Born in Ottawa in 1960, **Cameron Cardow** (Cam) attented Sheridan College in 1983, where he studied illustration. In 1984, he joined *The Citizen* in Ottawa as a staff artist and a year later was asked to submit one cartoon a week on a free-lance basis.

Born in Montréal in 1945 and having studied painting and graphic arts at l'École des Beaux-Arts, **Serge Chapleau** became an instant celebrity in Québec in 1972 with a weekly full-colour caricature for *Perspectives*. He joined *Montréal-Matin* two years later where he did editorial cartoons until the paper folded following a long strike. He regained stardom (or at least his voice did) when a puppet character of his, Gérard D. Laflaque became a suppertime regular on public TV. Despite huge ratings, the one-minute-and-fifteen-second daily program was deemed too sarcastic and was canceled after its first year. Serge resurfaced at the very sedate *Le Devoir* then quit for *Le Matin* a dynamic start-up which folded after less than two months. He now works at a Montréal TV station.

Mike Constable was born in Woodstock, Ontario in 1943. After studying sculpture at the Ontario College of Art, he moved on to Carlton University in Ottawa where he studied sociology. He was a co-founder of *Gorilla,* a Toronto underground newspaper from 1969 through 1974. In 1977 he was one of the founders of Union Art Services, a co-operative mailing service of graphics and cartoons, which presently goes out to about forty-five labour publications. Besides freelancing for *Saturday Night, TO Magazine, Canadian Tribune,* The Globe & Mail's *Report on Business,* he is editor of *Piranha* (Toronto's National Humour Magazine). He is presently spending the winter in Moscow, where he is teaching Russian cartoonists how to draw.

Born in 1948 in St. Thomas, Ontario, **Dale Cummings** studied animation and illustration at Sheridan College in Oakville. In 1974, he became one of the chief animators in the production of *True North,* the first successful attempt to include animated caricatures in a documentary film on Canadian politics and life. During a brief stay in New York he did some cartoons for *The New York Times.* He returned to Toronto in 1976, where he freelanced for *The Last Post, The Canadian Forum, Maclean's, The Toronto Star, Canadian Magazine* and *This Magazine.* Full-time editorial cartoonist with *The Winnipeg Free Press* since 1981, he won the National Newspaper Award in 1983.

LefT LoBe

THE OLD NEIGHBOUR-
HOOD HAD CHANGED

THE PROTECTIONIST:

STAND UP FOR AMERICA

Born Dec. 30th, 1958, **Fred Curatolo** published his first cartoon in the *Toronto Sun* in 1982. Since November 1986, he has been working for the *Brampton Guardian* and *Metroland* newspapers.

Anthony Delatri was born in Pennsylvania in 1922 and grew up in rural Québec, but returned to the US at the age of seventeen to join the army and served overseas during the Second World War. He studied later at the Newark School of Fine and Industrial Art, while drawing for several American publications. During this period, he also tried out as a pitcher for the New York Giants. By the 1950s, he was back in Québec. He did occasional drawings for *Le Journal de Montréal, Montréal-Matin,* and *Dimanche Matin* until becoming the full-time editorial cartoonist for *Le Nouvelliste* in Trois-Rivières in 1967.

Born in Montréal in 1949, **Susan Dewar** attended high school in Toronto, went to Western University, in London, and graduated from Toronto Teacher's College. In 1972 she travelled all over Europe and worked in Germany for two years as a tour guide. Back in Canada, she taught Cree children on native reserves and elementary grades in Toronto for two years. After working in commercial art and cartooning in Toronto, she started her company (Dewar's Ink) freelancing for *Canadian Forum, Bridges, Teen Generation Current* and the Toronto *Sun*. She joined *The Calgary Sun* as full-time editorial cartoonist in 1984.

Andy Donato was born in Scarborough in 1937. He graduated from Danforth Technical School in 1955 and began working at Eaton's as a layout artist. He left Eaton's in 1959 to join a small art studio and after a year decided to freelance. He joined the Toronto *Telegram* in 1961 as a graphic artist working in the promotion department. In 1963 he worked on the redesign of the paper and joined the editorial department. In 1968 he was appointed art director and began cartooning on a part-time basis. After the demise of the *Telegram* he joined the Toronto *Sun* as art director and produced two cartoons a week. In 1974, Donato took over cartooning on a fulltime basis. In 1985-86, he served as the second Canadian-born president of the Association of American Editorial Cartoonists.

Frank A. Edwards was born in Belleville, Ontario in 1940. After graduating from the Ontario College of Art, he worked as a commercial artist for several printing companies. In 1965, Frank accepted a position with Queen's University where he worked for 13 years as a medical illustrator. In 1978, he joined *The Whig Standard* in Kingston as its first full-time cartoonist. His work is syndicated in Canada and the United States.

Born in 1958, and after attending art school for two years, **Dave Elston** began freelancing full-time at the age of 21. One of his first breaks was doing a weekly sports cartoon for *The Calgary Sun*. He recently started his own sports cartoon syndicate, and in April of 1985 began filling in for Susan Dewar on the *Sun's* editorial page.

AT THE TIME, LEONARD THOUGHT IT A GOOD IDEA TO TRADE HIS OLD DOLLAR BILLS FOR THE NEW DOLLAR COINS...

Born in Texas in 1921, **Ed Franklin** started his career at *The Houston Press* in 1947 and, several years later, moved over to *The Houston Post*. In 1952, he went to New York to study at the Pratt Institute. In the fall of 1959, he visited Toronto and, feeling it would be a good place to bring up his kids, has been there ever since. First freelancing for *The Globe and Mail,* he then moved over to *The Toronto Star* for a while, filling in for Duncan Macpherson. In 1968, he moved back to the *Globe* alternating on the editorial page with Jim Reidford and became the daily cartoonist when Reidford retired in 1972. He won the National Newspaper Award in 1985.

Born in 1949 in Saskatoon, **Brian Gable** studied fine arts at the University of Saskatchewan. Graduating with a B.Ed. from the University of Toronto in 1971, he taught art in Brockville and began freelancing for *The Brockville Recorder and Times* in 1977. In 1980 he started full-time with *The Regina Leader Post* and is this year's National Newspaper Award winner.

"This one has half a mile on it. It was driven by a little old man in Windsor...

Born in Quebec City in 1954, **Serge Gaboury** started publishing cartoons at the age of 20. He has been drawing comic strips in *Croc* since 1979. Two collections of his work have since been published there: *La vie c'est mourant* and *Gaboury croque encore*. Besides working in animated films, he publishes sports cartoons in *Le Soleil* and does the editorial page drawing during Hunter's holidays. He has won two prizes at the Montréal International Salon of Caricature (1981 and 1982).

Born in Sault Ste. Marie in 1934, **Dick Gibson** has been working for the past 10 years at the *Toronto Sun* where both his political and situation cartoons have been featured. Right now his work appears across Canada and in some papers in the United States through Canada-Wide Feature Services. He has also been doing a drawing every week in the *Brampton Guardian* under the name of **Teasdale**.

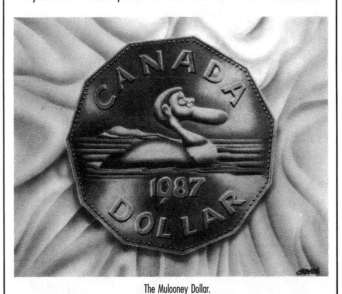

The Mulooney Dollar.

Jean-Pierre Girerd was born in 1931 in Algeria, where he studied art at l'École Nationale des Beaux-Arts for five years. In 1956 he was hired as a political cartoonist for the *Journal d'Alger*. In 1961 being a *pied noir* in Algeria was not very comfortable, so Girerd decided to move to the U.S., where he worked for *The Minneapolis Star* as a cartoonist and illustrator. Deciding that America was not for him, he settled in Paris. He came to Montréal on a holiday in 1964, and decided that he wouldn't mind living there, working in his native language. He worked for the newspaper *Métro Express* until it folded. After Berthio left *La Presse,* Girerd was hired as their editorial-page cartoonist and has been working there ever since. In 1985 he was named to the Order of Canada and won the Grand Prize at the Montréal International Salon of Caricature.

Mike Graston was born in Montréal in 1954. After graduating with an honors history degree from the University of Western Ontario, he was hired in a freelance capacity by the Ottawa *Citizen* in 1977. In January 1980, he moved to a full-time editorial cartooning position with *The Windsor Star*.

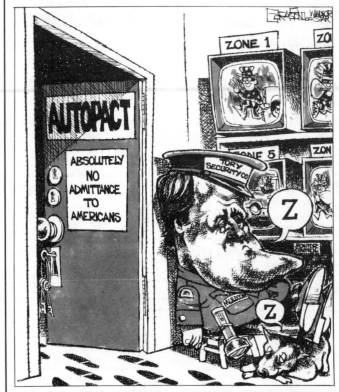

Born in Toronto in 1951, **Anthony Mark Jenkins** graduated in Arts from the University of Waterloo. His work has appeared in the *Globe and Mail* since 1974. He has travelled in 72 countries, on all continents but Antarctica, has published one book on these journeys, *Traveller's Tales*, and is currently at work on a second, *Somewhere Hot, Somewhere Not*. He needlepoints on Third World bus trips and ain't half bad at it. Father of Cayenne.

Born in Poland in 1923, **Jan Kamienski** studied art in Paris and Dresden and worked full-time in film animation. He came to Canada in 1949, and worked as commercial artist until 1958, when he joined the now-defunct Winnipeg *Tribune* until its closure in 1980. Since November 1980, he is staff cartoonist for The Winnipeg *Sun*. Over the years, he has won many awards including: City of Dresden Award for Graphic Work (1946), Art Directors Club of Toronto Award for Best Institutional Page (1957), Award of the Salon International de Caricature (1963), and National Newspaper Award for Editorial Cartooning (1964).

Jim Kempkes was born in Buffalo, New York, in 1947 and came to Canada in 1969. He studied fine arts at York University in Toronto where he was especially influenced by the drawing and sculpture of Honoré Daumier. Since then he has worked freelance, specializing in sculptural caricature in addition to contributing drawings to the Union Art Service and other publications.

Born in Belfast, Northern Ireland, in 1947, **Alan King** came to Canada with his family at the age of two. After graduating in English Literature from University of Western Ontario he taught high-school English, and worked as a piano salesman, a taxi driver, an engineering technician, an illustrator and an ad agency art director. Having studied classical music as a child and at the university level, he still plays as much piano as he has time for. Married, with one son, he has been with *The Citizen,* in Ottawa, since 1979 and is now doing five cartoons a week.

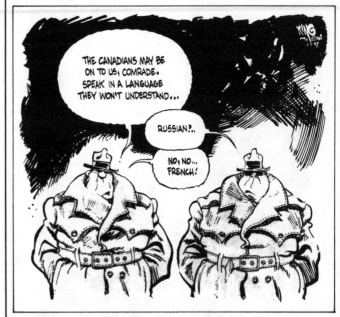

Barbara Klunder has been illustrating in Toronto for 20 years. Kid's books, record jackets, magazines, advertising. She also produces her own "politically correct" posters, rugs, fabrics, sweaters and T-shirts.

Born in Vancouver in 1954, **Bob Krieger** has been drawing political cartoons for *The Province* since 1981 where he now shares duties with illegal alien Dan Murphy. Krieger's work has also appeared in *Iaccoca, The Last Days of MASH, School Wars, The Expo Story* and *Bill Bennett: The End.*

Born in Swift Current, Saskatchewan in 1950, **John Larter** started at *The Lethbridge Herald* in 1974, went to *The Edmonton Sun* in 1978 and then to *The Toronto Star* in 1980.

Bruce MacKinnon, a native of Nova Scotia, grew up in Antigonish, N.S., studied fine arts at Mount Allison University, and was a member of the Graphic Design program at the Nova Scotia College of Art & Design. He started doing a weekly editorial cartoon with the *Halifax Herald* in 1985, working at home while raising his newborn daughter, Robyn. Through the miracle of daycare, he was able to join the *Herald* on a full-time basis in August of 1986, filling the void left by two-time National Newspaper Award winner, Bob Chambers.

Probably the most celebrated cartoonist in Canada, **Duncan Macpherson** was born in Toronto in 1924. Associated with *The Toronto Star's* editorial page since 1958, Macpherson has won the National Newspaper Award an unprecedented six times in 1959, '60, '62, '65, '70 and '72. In 1971 he received a $15,000 Molson Prize from the Canada Council, an honour presented for "a man's total career rather than any single work." In 1976 Macpherson was elected to the Canadian News Hall of Fame.

Phil Mallette was born in Sault Ste. Marie in 1955 but considers himself a native of Kirkland Lake, Ontario, where he grew up. After graduating from the University of Guelph in 1977 with a Bachelor of Arts degree in Fine Arts, he began working as a freelance cartoonist and illustrator in Toronto. When *Globe and Mail* cartoonist Tony Jenkins took an extended leave of absence in 1981 to travel, Phil sat in for him doing cartoons for the *Globe's* editorial page on Ed Franklin's days off as well as doing spot illustrations. Phil Mallette's cartoons appear regularly in *The Saturday Winnipeg Free Press* and *The Financial Post*. His work as illustrator has appeared in *The Financial Post Magazine, Canadian Business Magazine, Toronto Life, The Globe & Mail* and various other publications.

Malcolm Mayes was born in Edmonton, Alberta in 1962. After puberty and some encouragement from cartoonist Yardley Jones, he began to push a pencil on a regular basis. While studying Art at Grant Mac Ewan College, he started a company, Mayes Feature Service, to distribute his cartoons to publications across Alberta. He sold drawings to *The Calgary Herald, The Lethbridge Herald, Western Report* and *The Red Deer Advocate,* before starting as the editorial-page cartoonist for *The Edmonton Journal* in June 1986.

A full-time Toronto ad agency graphic artist, **Ken Munro** enjoys cartooning, illustrating, sandblasting design in glass, breaking 80, interesting winter velocities and a good laugh.

"MAKE MY DAY."

Dan Murphy was born in Missouri. He moved to Canada in the early seventies, drawing for various underground newspapers and aboveground magazines. He currently cartoons for the *Vancouver Province,* and the Rothco syndicate.

Len Norris was born in London, England in 1913 and moved with his family to Port Arthur, Ontario. He later moved to Toronto where he took night courses at The Ontario College of Art for one year. He worked as an art director for an ad agency from 1938 to 1940, when he joined the Army. For five years after the war he worked as an art director for Maclean-Hunter, working on various magazines, before heading out to Vancouver, where he had been offered a job at *The Vancouver Sun.* Norris won the National Newspaper Award the first year he entered, in 1951 and the *Sun* produced annual collections of Norris' cartoons for twenty-seven years. Eventually Norris became as much a symbol of BC as the totem pole. In 1973 the University of Windsor granted Norris an Honorary Doctorate of Law. Norris retired in 1978, but continues to draw two cartoons a week for the *Sun.* He has been elected to both the Canadian News Hall Fame and the Royal Canadian Academy of Arts.

"Aha! So you're the blighter who's been asking 40 percent of the Liberals, 31 percent of the NDPers, and only 29 percent of the Conservatives who they'd vote for..."

Born in Winnipeg in 1936, **Roy Peterson** works for *The Vancouver Sun* and *Maclean's* magazine and does occasional op. ed. page work for *The Toronto Star*. His work has appeared in all major Canadian and most major American newspapers and magazines as well as *Punch* and *The Spectator* in Britain. He has worked on newspapers, magazines and books as a team with Allan Fotheringham and with Stanley Burke on the bestselling *Frog Fables & Beaver Tales* series. Has illustrated many book covers and produced his own children's book *The Canadian ABC Book* as well as a collection of his cartoons *The World According to Roy Peterson* and *Drawn & Quartered*, a collection of editorial cartoons pertaining to the Trudeau years with text by Peter C. Newman. Married, with five children, he was, in 1982-83, the first Canadian-born president of the Association of American Editorial Cartoonists. He won the grand prize at the International Salon of Caricature in Montréal in 1973 and is three-time winner of the National Newspaper Award.

Roland Pier was born in France in 1936. He came to Canada in 1960, travelled extensively, and had various jobs including construction and working in a gold mine. Arriving in Montréal in 1962, he began freelancing and was eventually hired by *Le Journal de Montréal*. *Le Journal* has since become the largest French-language newspaper in North America. As Pier's cartoons also appear in a sister publication, *Le Journal de Québec*, he is undoubtedly the most widely read cartoonist in Québec today.

Born in 1935 in Hamilton, Ontario, **Denny Pritchard** worked in auto plants in Ontario. He began as free-lancer in 1975 and is now employed as staff cartoonist by the Saskatoon *Star Phoenix*.

Born July 1st, 1957, in Dunedin, New Zealand, **Adrian Raeside** got his start in cartooning, drawing on the back of bus seats on his way home from school. Moving to Canada in 1972, after a brief period in England, he worked at various jobs, from land surveying on the Northern BC coast, to unloading grain cars in a Thunder Bay grain elevator, before realizing he wasn't much good at any of them. Getting his first break in 1976, illustrating five children's books his mother Joan had written, he quickly became one of the most popular cartoonists on Wildwood Crescent and editorial cartoonist of the Victoria *Times Colonist* in 1980. As well as being widely syndicated in Canada, through his own syndicate, his work also appears in a number of U.S. publications. He has never won an award, and is not president of anything.

Born in Edmonton in 1946, **Vance Rodewalt** worked at *The Roughneck* after completing high school, where he did advertising cartoons. After working for Marvel Comics for 5 years, he travelled to Europe and, upon his return, began doing political cartoons for the Calgary *Albertan*. When the *Albertan* was bought by *The Calgary Sun,* he remained there for 3½ years before moving on to *The Calgary Herald* where he has been sharing editorial page cartooning duties with Tom Innes since the spring of 1983.

Vic Roschkov was born in Kiev in the Ukraine in 1941. After the war his family moved to Canada, eventually settling in the Windsor area. Roschkov developed a love of billiards while in high school and decided to drop out of the latter for the former. Hired in 1971 by the Windsor *Star* as editorial-page cartoonist. Five years later he moved to the *Toronto Star*, filling in for Duncan Macpherson on the editorial page. Leaving the *Star* in 1982, he freelanced for a couple of years before joining the *Edmonton Sun* where he has been the editorial-page cartoonist since 1984. He is also the winner of the 1980 National Newspaper Award.

WESTERN DIVERSIFICATION PACKAGE

Ting is the pen-name of **Merle Tingley,** political cartoonist for *The London Free Press*. Born and raised in Montréal, he studied art for one year and then worked briefly as a draughtsman until joining the army at the beginning of the Second World War. He began drawing cartoons on a full-time basis for the *Free Press* in 1948 and received the National Newspaper Award in 1955. He has now retired but still does two drawings a week on a freelance basis.

Jim Todd works as a self-syndicated freelance cartoonist for various newspapers in Atlantic Canada. He is a native of and presently resides in the small community of Perotte in southwestern Nova Scotia, and like most freelancers, is eventually hoping to work as a full-time editorial cartoonist for a daily paper. His cartoons have been published in a variety of Canadian and American political cartoon collections, as well as other publications and textbooks in the Maritimes and Ontario. His illustrations appear regularly in *Policy Options* magazine, published by the Institute for Research on Public Policy.

Since his debut at *The Edmonton Journal* in 1968, **Edd Uluschak**'s acclaim and popularity have been indisputable. Twice the recipient of both the National Newspaper Award for Cartooning and the Basil Dean Memorial Award for Journalistic Merit, Edd has also won many international awards and prizes. Edd, his wife Susan, their two children and his pet racoon now make their home on five acres of paradise on Gabriola Island, BC.

Born in London, England in 1926, **Ben Wicks** claims to have held the Nazi hordes at bay during the war as a swimming pool attendant at a Canterbury army camp. Having learned to play the saxophone in the army, he toured Europe with a band and was later to play in the orchestra on the liner Queen Elizabeth. Wicks moved to Canada in 1957, working as a milkman in Calgary. He sold several gag cartoons to *The Saturday Evening Post* and has never looked back. Moving to Toronto in 1960, he produces a daily syndicated cartoon (*Wicks*) in addition to his daily comic strip, *The Outcasts*. Organiser of the Thanksgiving African hunger relief effort two years ago he was, last year, named to the Order of Canada.

"With a home computer you can tell how much money you have in the bank at any time."

If you want to complete your **PORTFOOLIO** collection you are lucky. The first two issues are still available. To order, fill the form below (or a photocopy) and send it to:
CROC Publishing, 5800 Monkland Avenue, Montreal, Quebec H4A 1G1

... it's true... this guy I know down at the CBC says they often do re-runs of the weather picture in the summer... they think nobody notices...